Saint Martin Vésubie

No Approach, No Arriving

Andreas Müller

FSC
www.fsc.org
MIX
Papier aus verantwortungsvollen Quellen
Paper from responsible sources
FSC® C105338

Bibliografische Information der Deutschen Nationalbibliothek:
Die Deutsche Nationalbibliothek verzeichnet diese Publikation in der Deutschen Nationalbibliografie; detaillierte bibliografische Daten sind im Internet über www.dnb.de abrufbar.

Coverdesign:
Annemarie Nijenhuis & Wim Snijders

Herstellung und Verlag:
BoD – Books on Demand, Norderstedt

ISBN: 9783757818432

Contents

Amsterdam, October 2016

This is not about anything, so this event doesn't have a goal, it's not for anything, there isn't a real outcome. In that sense it really doesn't matter, that's the thing in advance. One could say there can't be a goal, it can't be for anything because that what happens is everything that is, and it's a part of the dream that there is something else. Or that there is another possibility, that there is a future, another level of something other than this. So, this is all there is, but this 'what is', can also appear as the sense of being someone. The sense of being a subject, something that is living here, in 'separation to the outside', or to something else outside. Concerning this message this is like a dream, it's not real. The sense of being a person isn't as real as it is experienced. This experience of being someone is based on the experience of reality and the experience of separation. So, within this setup it's absolutely real that I am real. That I am something 'in here', some instance, and that everything else is separate from me that is also real. So, there is a subject - object reality. And part of this dream 'I am' is the sense of time and space, of cause and effect, of good and bad, of meaning, of being a doer and of victimhood. 'I do things while other things happen to me', I am the experiencer. And part of that dream of being someone is the sense of being on a path, 'I am on my path in the future', and actually in a hopefully better future. If it works out very well in the moment the future can also remain like it is, but the idea is that the future is better. What also seems to be part of that setup of 'I am', is an unfulfillment. The sense that something is missing, that this 'what is', isn't whole. The sense is that somehow, something is missing. So, the 'me' begins to seek, that's the beginning of the seeking, and 'me' wants to find a way this can be whole for 'me'. Or, what can I do to experience this as whole, as absolutely whole without doubt. And it invents conditions, it has ideas about what should happen in order for this to be whole for me. So, I need more money, I need a better job, I need a partner, I need a better partner, I need different feelings, I need healing, I need insights, I need wisdom, I need enlightenment, I need the end of 'me', I need something. That's how me lives. Something should still happen in order for this to be whole. And then the apparent me starts working on its goal. So, it starts to be aware, it starts to heal, it goes on a career. And the sense is that I am personally responsible for my future luck, or enlightenment or goal of fulfilling. The dilemma is that the sense of 'I am', only consist of this. So, within this setup of 'I am' there is no finding. 'Me' only consists of being apparently separate, being unfulfilled, and seeking for oneness. It will not find, because within this setup there is no finding. Respectively one could say everything that me believes to find, like an insight, like more money, like the right partner, turns out to be unfulfilling as well. In the end one could say, it's unfulfilling because it's nothing real. So, within this setup of 'I am', there is no arriving, no finding, no solution. What we talk about here is the complete end of the experience of being a person and together with this end, together with this death, the whole dreamworld dies, it dies as well. So, what dies is separation, good and bad, cause and effect, right and wrong, sense, meaning. What dies with it, is the sense to be on a path, and what dies with it is the sense that something is lost, and that I have to find it again. In the end what dies is reality itself. The sense that something real exists dies. What is left is that what happens, what's left is this. Sitting and breathing, and looking, and a room, and a floor, chairs, thoughts maybe, feelings. That remains, and the surprising is without someone experiencing it, without this artificial reality one could say. It is everything, and by being everything, it's somehow whole and complete. But it is whole and complete as it is. There is no one experiencing whole and complete, there is no one who is aware of this being whole and complete. It just is whole and complete in a way as I said, it is whole and complete just by being everything. But in the same way it's also nothing, because when the dream of objects dies, that there are objects, you can't take out things any longer. So, this is nothing in the sense of: 'it's not this or this'. It's nothing in particular, it's just nothing and it's everything. So, there is no goal, there is nothing to get, this already is. I don't have anything to give, there is no message. Nothing will go from here to there, because what is, already is. So, we're not talking about something that will happen, we're talking about something that already is. That's why it's actually pointless.

Totnes, March 2017

The apparent special thing in this event is that there is no goal, no intention, no direction. One can say that the whole setup, the whole energetic setup 'in order to', that this speaking is in order to cause an effect or to cause a reaction, is illusory or in the end doesn't take place. What may take place is the illusion that this is for something else, this is what apparently happens, of course. Yet, all there is, is what happens. This is everything, so this can't possibly be for something else. For a future happiness, for a future enlightenment, for a better state. So, because this is all there is, this is everything, there can't be any help, or tips, or a path or methods. This is not coming out of an idea that it is better not to have paths, this is not an idea that this is a better help not to have paths or methods, it's just coming out of an impossibility; this is everything and there is nothing separate from this. So, there is simply no approach to this, there can't be, there simply isn't. It is part of an illusion, so to speak, and this illusion as we talk about is the sense of 'I am'. That's the dream, it's not the idea that 'I am'. As a description one could say, it's an energetic setup. It's really a feeling, a sense of I am something in here, something on my own, I am separate, 'I am'. The dilemma is that this 'I am' consist of 'I experience something', that's the basic thing how it lives. 'I am here and I experience this situation I am in, and those are two real things. And it seems to be within that setup there is an unfulfillment. Because I only experience the situation, which I am separate from. As this I am facing something alien and I have to behave myself towards it. And it seems to be that within that setup there is an unfulfillment. It doesn't have to be strong; it can be very subtle, but it's a sense of 'this just isn't everything'. Something still will come in the future, something is waiting in the future for me, and then it's really full or whole for me. And then I'm having an experience of fulfilment, of arriving, of finding, of silence, of relaxation. And that this only is the step to this future fulfillment. So, when 'me' is experiencing 'me', it lives in this 'I experience that this isn't it, but if I do behave in the right way this will lead me to fulfillment'. That's in a way how me lives. And that's its dilemma, that me only consist of living like that. It never reaches that point of arriving infulfillment, it's just not part of the setup, because the whole setup only consists of apparently being separate and seeking for what is. There it stops, it never comes to finding, it never comes to arriving, it never comes to that experience of lasting realisation that me is looking for. Because whenever there is me, there is the sense of unfulfillment, the sense of seeking. So, what we are talking about here, is not finding the 'right' way within that setup. Not the right way of 'what can I do or not do', or how can I find? It is not to find fulfillment within that setup of 'I am' and 'I experience something'. What we talk about here is that this whole setup, this whole energetic apparent ongoing isn't something real. There is no reality to it, and seen from the apparent me what we talk about is death. It's just the end of that sense of 'I am', it is not an understanding, it is not a realisation within that setup. It's just the end of that, seen from the me it's death. The surprising thing is that in dying, in the last exhalation so to speak, it becomes obvious that there isn't anyone alive to die. So even the story that there is an I that can die, even that is a story. So, in the end, in liberation, nothing happens. In the end there is no such thing as liberation. What's left in a way is what always was, it's what happens. What's left is what apparently happens, what's left is this. Sitting and breathing and a room and thoughts and feelings, it's this. And surprisingly without someone only experiencing, without someone artificially separated from it. It's whole and complete, it's everything, but there is no one left to notice that, there is no need to notice it either. So yeah, it's just this, because this already is it. There is no approach, I can't help, I can't give anything, nor take away anything. Nothing is too much here, and nothing is missing. It's this, exactly as it is, there isn't anything else, there just isn't.

Paris, April 2018

One of the special things about this is that I actually have nothing to say. So, I don't have anything to offer, I don't have good advice. I'm not helpful basically because there is no one to help, there is no one here who could help. This is all there is, there is nothing else so to speak. This isn't something that's moving into the future, it's just everything. This is just everything, there is nothing else. There is an apparent dilemma one could say, that's when 'that' happens as the sense of 'I am'. Which is an energetic experience so to speak. So, the experience is that I am something that is here; a person or consciousness. Christians would say the soul, the deepest inner. That's the dream, the dream that I am something that is in here in contrast to something that is out there. That's the dream, it's not a mental idea, it's a felt experience, this 'I am something'. So, one could say this setup is a dual setup. Or actually it's three; It's me, out there, and the perception in between these two, or the process of consciousness. Or how you want to call it. That's not right or wrong, that's just what apparently happens if it is what apparently happens. The apparent dilemma is that together with that sense of presence there is a sense of unfulfillment running with it. So, it's not just 'I experience something', but additionally 'what I experience, doesn't seem to fulfill me'. So, what 'me' is basically doing is trying to overcome that sense of unfulfillment. Or one could say the seeking energy comes out of this instantaneous sense of unfulfillment. The immediately experience is; 'this isn't it', I am sitting here now, and what I experience isn't everything. This is just a part of my life, which hopefully may lead me into a fulfilled future. So that's one could say how 'I am' lives. 'I have to behave in the right way now, in order to maybe arrive in a future fulfilled state'. The dilemma is that within that setup there is never an arriving, that fulfilled experience never happens. That final fulfilled experience never happens. Because whenever there is the sense of a person, the experience is that, 'this isn't it', and that I am only moving towards my goal. That's how me lives, that's what me is so to speak. That's kind of the bad news. The good news is that this whole structure so to speak, that this whole setup is illusory, or a dream. Which means that presence isn't real, the unfulfillment isn't real, and the need to fulfil that unfulfillment is a dream to. Seen from the me, what we talk about today, is just death. It's the end of that experience of 'I am something', that I am something that has an experience, that lives in a world, and has a task. The task of personal fulfillment so to speak. In that sense what we talk about is just death. But the surprise is that in dying, in 'actual' dying, it turns out that there is nothing there, it turns out that there is nothing that lives in the first place. Actually, there is nothing to die. And it turns out so to speak, that the whole presence of 'me', never really happened, it was never something real. So, in death nothing dies. What's left after death so to speak, after apparent dead, is just what happens. It's just this, and the surprise is one could say without anyone only experiencing it, without anyone separate from sitting in a room, it's just whole and okay and right. Beyond pleasant and unpleasant, but just right in its own way. So, what's left is this, that's everything, it's free and whole, there is no need for anything. There is no need for an additional realisation of that, there is no need for the seeing of oneness or something. There is no need at all, there is just sitting in a room. It's just this.

Helsinki, November 2018

So, I can start with good news. The good news is that what we talk about is very, very simple. That means it's as simple as there is nothing to gain. There is nothing to get out of this, or to reach, nothing to understand or to lose, or to intergrate, or to heal, or to anything. Basically, what is pointed to is that what happens, or what apparently happens is just everything. It's just already everything. And there is nothing additionally to reach or realise in that, this is everything and it's just whole and complete naturally. So, every idea of an additional realisation is just an illusion, it has no reality at all. The need to find something additional also has no reality at all. Apparently, one could say there can be that illusion, that's neither right nor wrong, it can't be prevented but it has no reality at all. Even if that is what apparently happens. So, in that sense this event or what we talk about is not a teaching. Because if this is everything, I can't tell you anything for an additional realisation. In that sense this is not a teaching. I can't teach anything, there is nothing to learn and there is no one to teach anything, and there is no one who needs to learn anything. All of that would be part of the dream, and what I would refer to as the dream here in this event today is the sense of 'I am'. The sense that I am someone, and the idea that I have to additionally find some fulfillment or realisation or a key to fulfilment, or the answer.

This whole assumption would be part of that dream of 'I am'. So, this whole thing is regarded as the dream or as an illusion. But even that is a story, because when I say that's an illusion, it actually means that there is not even something like that. So, in that sense me is not even an illusion, so when I say 'me is an illusion' it basically means that there is no me. It's just not there, it's not something that has a substance that is there. In that sense again this is all there is, and there is nothing additionally to reach or to get, or gain out of this. It's naturally whole and complete, sitting in a room is naturally whole and complete. But, and that's maybe the interesting thing for the 'me' so to speak, it's whole and complete for no one. Which means that there also is no additional experience of this being whole. It just is whole, but no one notices it. Because exactly the noticing of it, or the assumption of a noticing of it would be the additional realisation, which again has no reality at all. So, all of this 'aah I understand', all of 'I can see it', and all of 'aah it's this', would be illusionary. It's completely illusionary and not needed at all. Sitting in a room doesn't need this 'aah, I am whole actually'. It doesn't need that at all. It's just the illusion of self-awareness. It's just the illusion of 'I am something', which desperately longs for this additional; 'yeah, but I have to see it', 'but I have to become fulfilled'. Nothing else does that. No chair does that, no room does that, no cushion, not anything. No thought, no feeling lives in the dream of needing something else. It's just this sense of, this notion of self-awareness, this notion of 'I am separate'. Liberation, which is a strong word because liberation doesn't exist, but liberation as we talk about today would be just the breakdown of that experience of 'I am someone'. It would be just the end of that for no special reason. Not because it's right, not because it's something that is worldwide to achieve for anyone. But liberation in that sense is just the end of that setup, and automatically the end of that additional need. And the surprise is, one could say for no one, is exactly what I started with. What is; sitting in a room is just naturally whole and complete and doesn't need anything. This doesn't need any additional realisation so to speak. And that's the simplicity, it simply is like that one could say. Nothing has to be done, nothing can be done. Seen from the me this is an impossible message. Because it's impossible to do it's impossible to realise, it's impossible to additionally see it. In that sense it's an impossible message. It's impossible to reach by simply already being it, that's the simplicity. In that sense I have nothing to say, there is no one to help. This is it.

New York City, March 2019

This is all there is, there is nothing to realise, there is no additional realisation to what apparently happens. So, one could say what apparently happens is the perfect realisation already, it's perfectly realised, it's totally and perfectly and utterly itself. There is no 'second' reality so to speak to what is. In a way 'what is' in that sense also, is not a reality. It is no-thing, one could say. It's not really a circumstance which can be known or experienced, or understood, or felt, or any of that. Because one could say it's just whole, there are no separated objects, there are no separate entities, there are no paths. Or, one could say it in another way; the only thing which experiences itself to be apart is the me. Nothing else has an experience 'to be', so to speak. No chair, no whatever, nothing else has an additional experience 'to be'. Everything just is what it is and the only illusion of knowing what's going on comes from awareness. From the illusion that I am something that's here, which is only aware or which is only experiencing everything else. That's not bad, so to speak. Or that's not right or wrong, in the end it does not even really happen. But the apparent dilemma in the sense the 'me' would understand it, which also isn't bad, the apparent dilemma is that it seems that the sense of presence, or this experience of awareness seems naturally to be accompanied by a sense of unfulfillment. Or, that 'I am here', 'I'm experiencing this' and something seems to be missing. As a story one could say presence is unpleasant, the experience to be present seems to be unpleasant in some way or the other. The good news is, or what's being said here is that this whole setup, this whole experience to be present is a dream. Which means it doesn't happen, it's not there, it's a dreamt reality, an artificial reality that has no reality at all. That means that the whole sense of unfulfillment has no reality at all, and automatically the whole need to fill that whole, the whole need to become fulfilled also is only part of that dream. There just is nothing that has lost something, there just is nothing who needs something. It's just not there, it's an imagined reality.

In that sense, this is not a teaching at all. This is not speaking to that assumed person to show the way. To show what to do so to speak. What apparently happens is a pointing that this setup does not exists. That's what apparently happens without an intention, without the idea that this is useful, without the idea that this is for a better circumstance. One could say the pointing itself is already itself, is already complete by being itself. Not knowing itself of course. In that sense this is it. This is absolutely it, there is noting else. This is not in order to, it's this, surprisingly and amazingly exactly as it is.

Toulouse, June 2019

Bonjour, hello, guten Tag. So, apparently one interesting thing about this event is that it's absolutely for nothing. This means that there is no additional goal in it. We are not meeting here in order to create something else. A feeling, an experience, a new way of thinking, there is literally no goal in this. What is, or what apparently happens is everything and is naturally whole and complete. So, there is no additional realisation to this. Sitting in a room, being you, being me, being chairs, being thoughts and feelings is so to speak one hundred percent realised. This is everything, exactly as it is. The whole idea that there is something like an additional realisation to this, namely something like: 'I have to see this', or 'I have to become aware of this', or 'I have to arrive in that and consciously feel it', and those kind of things. They all belong to the dream one could say. And the dream in that sense would be the illusion, the experience to be something. A person, a human being, consciousness, awareness, to be something which is present. All of that would be seen as the dream, and one could say the basic setup is the experience of separation, of two. Because, as soon as you have one, one thing, there is something around it. So, one is automatically two. And that's the basic experience of the person, there is something which I am, and there are a lot of other things which I am not. But I really exist, and all those other things, which I am not, also really exist. This is the basic setup of the person. This setup is an illusion by the way, it doesn't exist. So, it's a bit funny to talk about. This whole setup is not wrong, but there is an apparent dilemma coming with it, so to speak. It seems to be that that which experiences itself as 'me' or 'this', is somehow unfulfilled and seeks for fulfillment in the second. That means, the first is looking in the second. That's basically what it means to live as a person, or to be a person. To be something which is constantly seeking for fulfillment, in what it experiences, in what it is aware of. That's basically the personal life. Within that setup, there is never an arriving, there is never an experience of an end of that, there is never an experience of fulfillment which is final, or which lasts. Because the mere existence of that presence so to speak, is the apparent cause for the unfulfillment in the first place. So, whenever the apparent me believes to do or not do, it of course will never lead beyond me. Me only knows me. Me only knows itself and how it is to experience. Me only knows the dream and thinks its reality. So, what we talk about today 'apparent liberation' seen from the me, is the end of me, it's death. And in the end, it's death for no reason. And not because I did already this and that, and know that, the end of me has nothing to do with what 'me' thinks where it's at. Death doesn't have conditions. But even this whole 'me dying thing' of course is a story. Because in dying it turns out that there is nothing there alive in the first place. There is no individual, there is no such thing as 'me and my life'. It's not real, and it never was real, so to speak. So, in death, in dying, nothing actually happens. The whole idea that I am happening, or the experience that I am happening, doesn't and didn't have any substance at all. So, in life so to speak, there is nothing in there which is alive. And in liberation, in death, there is nothing in there which is dead or liberated. What's left so to speak after dying, which is a joke, is what apparently happens. And surprisingly, it's completely and totally naturally whole and complete. But of course, for no one. Which means that there is nothing sitting 'in' the wholeness, experiencing it. There is nothing sitting in the wholeness, being aware of it. In that sense, this is it, there is nothing to get, there is no one separated, nothing is lost, nothing has to be found. Which turns this into something very simple. It's this.

Brighton, April 2022

So, the good thing about this event is that there is no goal in this. It's really not about anything. And it can't be about anything, because what happens or what apparently happens is just this, so to speak. And it's naturally whole and complete, it's everything in that sense. There is not a deeper goal, or a deeper reality or something like that, it's just this. What happens, what apparently happens, is just itself so to speak. That's the natural reality. And any idea, any assumption that this is happening for something, any assumption that there is a deeper reality, or an absolute reality or stuff like that is just coming from a dream. And the dream in that sense would just be 'I am'. The assumption that there is an entity living in this body, which we 'really' are, that there is something who we are. That's the dream, that's the illusion. And I know, when I call it an illusion it may sound a little bit superficial, like an idea or a concept or something. But no, for the person it's really its sense of existence, that's the dream. For the person it really feels as if 'I am a real entity that is now here, experiencing a real situation'. But it's exactly this impression that 'I'm now here', that there is something real going on, which doesn't have any substance at all. And all the ideas that come out of this impression. Like; 'I have an autonomous existence, I am separate from wholeness, I have lost something, I am on a path through life and I am on a path back to wholeness'.

This is all part of the dream, it's all the same dream, it's based on 'I am', 'I exist'. And also, when I say it's a dream, I don't mean that it is something that we now have to work on, or get rid of. It basically means that there isn't anyone in the first place. There is just no one here, there is nothing to teach, there is nothing that I could say or give or take away, and there is no one there also who could take something or who needs to get rid of something. That's what's meant when is said that this is all there is, and when is said this is perfect, whole and complete. It's just this, all there is, is what apparently happens. And it's naturally fine. There is no possibility of any additional realisation, there is no one there who will ever notice, recognise this, arrive in this, who will find this. It does not exist; it can't happen because there is no one in the first place.

Germany, October 2022 - OnenessTalks, broadcasted online by Jetzt-TV

A warm welcome to this talk, maybe briefly what will happen this afternoon. I willmake a little introduction to what we're roughly talking about. Then there may be questions or comments, and of course, if no one comes up with something it may also be silent. This is not about anything, that's ultimately the good news and ultimately not only here in this talk but in life « in general ». And what is being said here is that this very life so to speak, which the person assumes exists, does not exist, there is no one at all. That's one thing which is pointed out. This self-experiencing, to experience yourself as something, feels from the person's point of view as absolutely real. The person would always say 'I'm here, I'm here now, I am aware, I am aware of what's happening'. When I say 'there is no one' this refers exactly to this feeling. It has no substance at all, it doesn't exist. And with that, automatically all the consequences resulting from this experience do not exist. And the consequences, in quotation marks, can be a feeling of search, that something is lost, that something is missing on a very basic level, and that this absence somehow must be fulfilled. That you have to do something to fulfill yourself as 'I', and that therefore exists the right way to live, or the right way to be. This is ultimately the personal experience. That'swhat it feels like to be as: 'I am now here and I have to act to become something'. In this gathering this could be « following those words », or something like this. Listening to Andreas and following those words, hoping this brings me something like an added value, that there exists an added value. That's one side, referring to exactly this experience that has no substance whatsoever. That's the one illusion and the one and only illusion as it were. This investigation, the investigation of the person is of course doomed to failure. There is no possibility to fill this felt hole, there is no possibility to answer this feeling of loss, this pain of separation one could say. There is for the person no possibility to heal this. Ultimately because the person itself is the reason for this. This means whenever I believe I am one step further, or I have achieved something, I'm already there again to reject it. To say it's still not enough, I have understood something about life, but it's just 'I' who understood something, and again 'I' will be there to say to this understanding 'this wasn't it, this wasn't all'. When this experience of being someone turned out to be an illusion, as absolutely without substance, with that the experience of being insufficient disappears. This just belongs together, not because it's being answered, not because the search ever worked out, not because the whole search has paid off, but completely surprisingly it simply vanishes with it. It was part of the dream, this felt longing for unity, for wholeness, for goodness, was simply part of an Illusion. And the surprise is when it's gone as it were, (this as a very simplified story), when it's gone the surprise is that what's happening is naturally okay. It's normal and it is normal that it is in harmony and okay, however for no one. Which means there is no one left experiencing this being okay or must experience it. What we're talking about is a blind okayness. There is simply no problem, there is nothing deeper to find, no one has lost anything. And because it already is the case, it isn't learnable. One could also say that as what's happening is wholeness, it's not achievable. Ultimately, achieving always involves the idea of a later ahead, that at some point this will be the case. No, it won't be like that someday, that's part of the dream, that's it. There is only that which apparently happens, and it's naturally whole and complete, exactly so. It will never become more whole, it will never become more complete, it will never become essential, truer, whatever the person is looking for. More fulfilling or whatever, it doesn't exist, it will never be the case and doesn't have to. Insofar this is really not about anything this afternoon. This is not somehow an attempt in a roundabout way to make this about something after all. No one will achieve anything today, no one will lose something, it's simply this. Timeless, spaceless, unknown in a way and yet simply this. There's no more.

Verona, October 2022

Okay, let's start, welcome everyone. This is not a teaching, there isn't anyone here, and there isn't anyone over there. That's what's being pointed out here for no reason, it doesn't have any intention. So the pointing out of that, is what apparently happens. That's wholeness already, it doesn't want to produce a result. That's what I mean when I say there is no intention. In that sense one could say this message just points to itself. It's sitting in a room, saying 'I am all there is'. But again, that's just what apparently happens. And it's unknowable, and its whole and complete. So, what's also being pointed out here is that there is no 'I', there is absolutely no separate entity at all. And I don't mean this in a philosophical or conceptual way. In a way this experience to be someone, this felt sense of presence doesn't have any reality. And all ideas of personal fulfillment are also part of that dream. So, in that sense this is also not a spiritual message. Because how I would see it, so to speak, all spirituality is trying to make this in a spiritual fulfillment. So, in that sense this here is also not spiritual. So liberation, which is a story, isn't something that happens to the person. It's not something that happens within a personal story. It's the collapse of this sense of 'I am', or actually the apparent collapse of the illusion of being a person. It doesn't need anyone, there isn't anyone left after that so to speak. There isn't any kind of experience left. And what's left is what apparently happens, which is inexperienced and unknown, and it's naturally whole and complete. It's this, it's just this. So, this can't be taught, what apparently happens can't be taught, and it doesn't need to be learned. That's it.

Asheville March, 2023

This doesn't happen for anything or for any deeper reason. What I do, apparently, is just this apparent pointing to that this is whole and complete already, and there's absolutely nothing to gain or to achieve. This whole idea that there is something to achieve is part of a dream, that life is about something. That something deeper is going on that we don't see, or that we don't experience, is part of a dream. And the dream is 'I am', 'I exist'. The sense to be something that is now here, something that's aware of itself. This is what I would call the illusion, and it's the only illusion. There is no other illusion than 'I am here', 'I am a separate entity that has an experience of itself' so to speak. And all the ideas about becoming something, about finding something deeper, about finding the purpose of life or the meaning of live or becoming an enlightened person, or a fulfilled person so to speak, all those ideas only happen within that illusion. These ideas only happen for this illusion of self-awareness. 'I am a self that's aware', 'I have a conscious experience of myself and a separate world'. There is nothing wrong with that, but what seems to be a part of that experience to be someone is this sense of lack, as if something is missing. As if what I'm aware of now is just not fulfilling, as if it's not everything. So that's where the seeking comes from. The seeking for more peace, more love, more clarity, more fulfillment, less me, less struggle, less problems, less unclarity or whatever. This is all part of the thing. So, what this points to is basically that. There is no one there in the first place. This I which assumes to be separate, which assumes that something is missing, this I isn't real, this I doesn't have any substance. So, no one has lost anything, no one needs to find something, no one needs to become aware of another or deeper reality, it's all just part of a dream. This is all there is, it's this. This is the natural reality and it's whole and complete already, for no one of course.

But who cares, I mean there's no one there in the first place. What we talk about here, or what this point to basically is that what happens or what seems to be happening is everything. And when I say it's everything, I mean it in a sense that it's whole and complete. There is no hidden reality like a meaning or purpose, or there is no absolute reality where this is coming from, or a source or something. No, this is everything that happens, what seems to be happening is just everything. It's itself one could say, sitting in a room is itself, so that's all there is. The other thing that we talk about, or the other thing that this point to is that there is no separate entity, there is no experience. This sense to be something on its own, 'me', some kind of entity, this impression is completely illusory. There isn't anyone, that's what's meant when I say that there is no one, there is no 'me', there is no one. It refers to this artificial sense of presence. This doesn't exist, and all ideas about finding something deeper, all ideas that life has a purpose, or that there is a goal in life, or that this event has a goal, or that it's somewhere leading somewhere, this whole impression is part of that dream. So, basically the dream is; 'I'm now here, I'm experiencing this, something is missing and I'm on a path towards the actual thing.' This whole bundle so to speak is the illusion, it all goes together. 'I'm separate, I'm now here, I'm on a path, something's missing and fulfillment will still come for me.' Hopefully of course, but that's the dream. And in the story one could say, 'liberation', I know it's a weird word anyway, but liberation in that sense would just be the collapse of that impression to be a separate entity. It's not a realization, it's not an understanding, it's not another experience, it's just the collapse of the illusion of experiencing. And what's left, apparently one could say, is just what's happenning. It's sitting in a room, it's breathing, it's thinking, it's feeling, it's the room, or whatever seems to be happening. And it's naturally whole and complete, but it's also ordinary and empty and meaningless. That's the natural reality, it's just this.

There is no achievement, there is no arriving in that, there is no one awaking to the natural reality or something. It's just the collapse of the illusion of separation.

St. Martin Vésubie May, 2023

What we do here is actually quite direct, apparently. So, we very directly point out what happens is all there is, that what happens is the natural reality, that's just naturally everything and that's just naturally itself. And what we also talk about, or what this also points out, let's say very directly, is that there is no separate entity, there is no experience of. That's basically the illusion, that's basically the only illusion, that there is a separate entity called me or awareness or consciousness or that's called the soul or some kind of spirit that lives within us. Those would all be names for the same thing, the impression that there is something in the body which we really are. That's the dream basically what this message points out, and in the end the only thing it points out is that; 'hey there is no one', apparently. And all the questions, the whole seeking drive, the drive to find something deeper in this moment, or in live in general, belongs to that illusion if you want. So, it's just one bundle of things, the impression to be something, the impression to be separate, the impression to have lost something. Something very basic so to speak, some basic peace, some basic trust, some basic happiness. That that's lost is part of that impression to be separate, and to the impression to be on a path back to that holiness or love, or freedom, or total trust, or whatever is sought, kind of. It's basically this feeling, this feeling of well- being, the experience of 'I can just be without the need to seek'. That's basically what is sought within that setup. And all the things that I just said are part of this one dream so to speak. Those aren't even really aspects that can be separated from each other and worked through little by little, it's just one bundle. So, the moment you have the illusion of self-consciousness or self-awareness, you have somehow all those ingredients. The sense of reality, having lost something, the need to seek, hopes, dreams, the illusion of failure of course on that path, the suffering, frustration, desperation that comes from that impression; 'I can't make it, I'll never make it'. Those are all ingredients of that dream and the basis of that dream is 'I am', 'I exist', I'm separate. So, what usually this personal life is about, is; 'what's the right path'. That's the only question the person lives in, 'how should I be, how should I do', what's the right way to be in order to become a fulfilled me. That's the seeking, and in a way that's the only question the person has, in the end it boils down to that. And usually within the person's life that's what life seems to be about, to do the right things to be in the right way. Or at least to not be in the wrong way, or to not do the wrong things. Of course this doesn't work out, because it's all within the experience of the person and the experience itself is the experience of unfulfillment. So, nothing works, no path works, no methods work, no attempt to be in the right way works. And what this is about, what we talk about here is not another idea on how to be, it's totally impossible for me to suggest another path, or I don't have another, a new idea on how anyone should be. This would just be part of the same dream. What this point's out is that this whole bundle is illusory, and in the story we could say right now, already. It's not that this will be discovered at some point in the future, there already isn't anyone, it's already illusory, it's already without any substance. There is no path, there is no step that we take together here for example. There is nothing that's lost and there's nothing that's needs to find it's way back to wholeness and become aware of it, no separated something is lost. Of course, seen from the person separation is not just a concept, it really seems to feel like that. But it's exactly that sense of presence, that felt sense of 'I exist', 'I am something', which doesn't have any substance at all. No matter how it calls itself, awareness or presence or 'I am a spirit', an entity, a soul, or a contracted energy, the seeking energy, whatever. There is no such thing, it's purely illusory let's say. And that's why there is no message or teaching, it's not coming out of an understanding, it's not a dogma like 'there can't be a teaching' or something. When this energetic dynamic of being someone drops, of being a seeker, or the illusion to be someone turns out to be illusory, it's just impossible to teach anyone, or to know anything.

I mean the opposite of teaching would be knowing anything like; 'I'm not anyone who's been used to be taught', 'I am someone who knows already'. Both are illusory, there is no one, there's just no one there. So, that's it. What seems to be happening is everything, there won't be any additional realization ever, a moment in time when it will feel really more whole and complete than it does now. There won't be a future experience which will be the final experience. There is no reality that's called experiencing, it doesn't happen. It's this setup 'I am', 'I exist', 'I am aware of' and 'I am aware of something' which doesn't exist. There's no separation at all.

About Andreas Müller

Andreas was born in 1979 in Ludwigsburg in Southern Germany. After years of seeking in spirituality, he met Tony Parsons in 2009.
"First, I was shocked. Though I had already known and experienced a lot, this was something new and unexpected. Suddenly, for no reason, I heard what Tony was saying, and soon it was undeniable: There is no one."
Since 2011, Andreas has been holding talks and intensives throughout the world.

www.thetimelesswonder.com

About Saint Martin Vésubie

The last written introduction was given during a holiday intensive in Saint Martin Vésubie, located in the South-East of France. Approximately one hour north of Nice. Being situated in the French Alps, it is surrounded by a wonderful landscape of mountains and forest. The weather there can be very changeable, fog, sun and rain, even snow on top of the mountains, all can appear during the same day.

The meetings with Andreas were given in a beautiful eco Lodge, a so-called organic guest house, the Moonlight Chalet.

Great thanks goes to

Wim Snijders for the setting up this book

Annemarie Nijenhuis & Wim Snijders
for the cover design

Benoît Strauss & Maëlle Le Berre
for setting up the intensive in St. Martin Vésubie

Vivien Thomas

Tony & Claire Parsons

My family

Books that have been published by Andreas in English:

No-thing – ungraspable freedom

You will never be free
questions and answers on non-duality

Unlocked
Bondage and Liberation The end of all Lockdowns

No-Point Perspective

No-Point

Taverna Lentas
Talks Around Closing Time

One Seeing, One Knowing, One Love
Andreas Müller on Master Eckhart